THIS JOURNAL BELONGS TO:

_____

BEST

WORST

GRATEFUL

5-Minute
Mindfulness Journal

SPRUCE BOOKS

A Sasquatch Books Imprint

The Transformative Power of a Daily Review and a Moment of Gratitude

*Whatever a person frequently thinks
and ponders upon, that will become
the inclination of their mind.*
—BUDDHA

It seems that lately everyone is talking about the many benefits of mindfulness or citing headlines about how practicing gratitude can improve your health and wellness. You may even have said to yourself, "I'm definitely going to meditate, become more mindful, and practice gratitude," only to find that you don't quite know how to start, or that it's hard to find the time or place to sit quietly, or that when you do find a moment, some other urgent task immediately presents itself. Before you know it, you are up and back in the fray, telling yourself you will come back to this whole mindfulness business some other time.

What Is Mindfulness? Why Gratitude?

Simply put, mindfulness is the ability to fully inhabit the moment you are in without judgment or criticism of what is happening, neither anticipating what's coming next nor regretting the past, not dreaming about being elsewhere, but rather living your own experience in the moment. It sounds simple but is actually challenging, as we are constantly distracted by phones and other attention-hungry devices; by worries, fears, and other strong emotions; by the pressure of obligations partially completed or that we know are waiting—the parade of distractions can be endless. Multitasking is the enemy of mindfulness.

Learning to focus on the moment offers us a powerful break from the constant stream of distracting thoughts (sometimes called "the monkey mind") that tends to be our regular state of consciousness. Studies show that learning to be mindful improves our ability to focus, helps us to feel less anxious, and can even have physical benefits such as lowering blood pressure and improving sleep.

Gratitude, defined even more simply, is the feeling of thankfulness and pleasure that we enjoy when we appreciate something in our lives. You may feel gratitude as a quick jolt of delight or a more complicated state with elements of acceptance, gratefulness, and even awe. Regardless of the mix, you know it when you feel it, and it feels good. Fortunately, you do not have to wait for gratitude to find you, because you can cultivate this feeling and experience it often.

How do you choose to experience gratitude? By focusing your attention on what gives you joy. The more you consciously practice this, the easier it becomes, and ultimately, you can train your mind to gravitate naturally to this positive feeling. Turn to the end of this introduction for gratitude exercises (page vi) that you can use to practice building your gratitude muscles.

Done regularly, a gratitude practice can help you to

- *let go of toxic emotions*
- *become less reactive and, instead, be more thoughtful and responsive*
- *feel greater empathy and more connected to other people*
- *lighten your mood*
- *feel less burdened by your obligations and challenges*

You know that mindfulness and gratitude can be transformative. How can you make it happen?

How to Use This Book

Best Worst Grateful offers a framework for a simple practice that requires just five minutes a day yet will transform your outlook and help you become calmer, more focused, more content, and even more joyful.

Set aside five minutes toward the end of your day—it could be when you sit down to eat dinner, just before you get ready for bed, or even when you finally climb under the blankets—any time that you can pause and take five minutes to reflect. (Tip: put it in your calendar.)

Step 1: Review

Take a moment to breathe and center yourself. Now, gently cast your mind back to when you woke up today and play back the events of the day like a movie. Do not judge yourself or others, resist the urge to grade yourself on your performance, and do not give in to the temptation to relive the emotions of the moment; simply move through the day, observing without mental comment. When you've done that, note the best thing that you experienced—the high point of your day. Next, note the worst thing—an experience that was unsatisfying or upsetting. The idea is not to linger, but rather to acknowledge each moment, understanding that every day must have both good and bad. No day, and no life, is made up of only great or awful moments—one cannot exist without the other, and both have lessons to offer you. Briefly, celebrate the good moment and resolve to learn from the bad moment. Now, let them both go.

Step 2: Be Thankful

Take another breath. You are already feeling calmer, having let go of the day's details. With all of the day now resting comfortably in your mind, choose an aspect of it for which you can feel a sense of gratitude. It doesn't have to be connected to either your best experience of the day or your worst; it needn't be profound—it just has to be something for which you can feel genuinely thankful. Your moment of gratitude may be as simple as recalling a smile shared, the warmth of sunshine on your face, a loving greeting from your pet, or a task well done. Or perhaps you are just grateful that whatever moment of unpleasantness you endured today is now behind you. Maybe you are grateful to have learned something, even if it was a bittersweet lesson. Whatever it is, take a moment to acknowledge and savor it, and think consciously to yourself, "I am grateful for _____." Sit with that feeling and savor it for a minute. When you've done that, you can finish your practice by taking one last deep inhalation and a slow exhalation. That's it!

This seemingly simple practice can have a dramatically transformative effect on your attitude, creating greater feelings of positivity, satisfaction, well-being. Studies show it also improves your ability to concentrate, and may help you to rebound more quickly when facing stress. The purpose of this book is to help you to make gratitude practice a regular part of your life.

Best Worst Grateful features undated pages, so you can use this book on your own schedule with no pressure to do it every single day.

Inspiring quotes are included throughout the book to help motivate you. And when you read or hear something that you find inspiring, jot it down and create your own collection of meaningful quotes. They will be an ongoing source of support for you. Practicing the gratitude exercises (page vi) will help you focus your attention on the aspects of your life for which you feel thankful and strengthen your ability to feel gratitude.

Use Best Worst Grateful to train your brain in the "attitude of grati-tude," an approach to living that puts gratitude in the forefront—and let it help you to enjoy the profound pleasures of a more mindful life.

25 Exercises to Build Gratitude Muscles

For many of us, being grateful is something we do not feel naturally good at. If you are someone for whom feeling grateful does not come easily, it's important to know that you can change that. You may be out of practice, because you have never thought about your experiences that way or because you simply have not had enough time or opportunity to try it. You may even have been cultivating an attitude of cynicism, anger, or some other negative approach in the belief that it could protect you. By choosing to practice gratitude instead, however, you can change your habits of mind. Here are a variety of ways to think about your experiences and ideas that can help you to get in the habit of feeling grateful. See which ones work best for you, and add your own. The more you practice feeling gratitude, the easier and more natural it will become.

- Was someone kind to you today? How did that make you feel?

- Did you take the opportunity to be kind to someone else? How did it make you feel?

- Did you learn something today? Reflect on that lesson.

- Think of a moment when you felt brave. Remember and sit with that feeling. Try to summon your bravery at other times.

- Find compassion for someone who annoyed or upset you today. Try to let go of any lingering ill-feeling. Is there anything you can learn from this interaction?

- When you are outdoors in a natural setting, pause and listen to the sounds of nature. Hold onto that feeling.

- Aromas can be powerful. Think of something that smelled good to you today. Can you intentionally bring into your day scents that make you feel good?

- Pause and breathe deeply for a full minute, exhaling more slowly than you inhale. Let calm fill you with each breath in and let and anxiety depart with each breath out.

- Did you receive a compliment today? Did you give one? Take pleasure in giving and receiving unexpected appreciation.

- Think of someone in your life whom you take for granted. What would you miss about that person were they not in your life?

- Did someone thank you today? How did it make you feel? Did you thank anyone else? If you think of someone you could have thanked but didn't, resolve to thank them tomorrow.

- Think of a place that you find unpleasant, ugly, neglected, or even frightening. Find something hopeful there.

- Think of something delicious you tasted today. How did that moment of enjoyment impact your day?

- What is a quality you appreciate in yourself? Think about how that characteristic helps you and others.

- Reach out to a friend with a specific appreciation for something you love about them and a thank-you for their friendship.

- Recall a happy moment from your childhood and let the feeling wash over you.

- Did something or someone make you laugh today? Remember and relive that moment of lightheartedness.

- Think of a quality that you value in someone you don't like. Can you focus on that instead of the negative?

- Remember something a parent gave you—a quality, a gift, a lesson, a compliment—that has made your life better.

- Think of a quality you value in someone close to you. Plan to let them know how much you appreciate it.

- Take a walk. Focus your attention on the motions of walking and enjoy the feeling of movement.

- What role does music play in your life? Consider the pleasure you have gotten from listening to your favorite songs or musicians.

- The next time you take a bath, shower, or swim, pause to enjoy the feeling of being immersed in or showered with water. Think about the connection between water and your well-being.

- Think of a book, movie, play, or other entertainment that has had a positive influence on you, and recommend it to someone else.

- Did someone help you out today? How did that make you feel? Look for an opportunity to help out someone else tomorrow.

DATE _____

THE BEST MOMENT OF MY DAY: _____

_____

_____

THE WORST MOMENT OF MY DAY: _____

_____

_____

TODAY I FELT GRATEFUL FOR: _____

_____

_____

_____

DATE _____

THE BEST MOMENT OF MY DAY: _____

_____

_____

THE WORST MOMENT OF MY DAY: _____

_____

_____

TODAY I FELT GRATEFUL FOR: _____

_____

_____

_____

DATE _____

THE BEST MOMENT OF MY DAY: _____

_____

_____

THE WORST MOMENT OF MY DAY: _____

_____

_____

TODAY I FELT GRATEFUL FOR: _____

_____

_____

_____

DATE _____

THE BEST MOMENT OF MY DAY: _____

_____

_____

THE WORST MOMENT OF MY DAY: _____

_____

_____

TODAY I FELT GRATEFUL FOR: _____

_____

_____

_____

DATE _____

THE BEST MOMENT OF MY DAY: _____
_____
_____

THE WORST MOMENT OF MY DAY: _____
_____
_____

TODAY I FELT GRATEFUL FOR: _____
_____
_____
_____

DATE _____

THE BEST MOMENT OF MY DAY: _____
_____
_____

THE WORST MOMENT OF MY DAY: _____
_____
_____

TODAY I FELT GRATEFUL FOR: _____
_____
_____
_____

DATE _____

THE BEST MOMENT OF MY DAY: _____

_____

_____

THE WORST MOMENT OF MY DAY: _____

_____

_____

TODAY I FELT GRATEFUL FOR: _____

_____

_____

_____

DATE _____

THE BEST MOMENT OF MY DAY: _____

_____

_____

THE WORST MOMENT OF MY DAY: _____

_____

_____

TODAY I FELT GRATEFUL FOR: _____

_____

_____

"Piglet noticed that even though he had a Very Small Heart, it could hold a rather large amount of Gratitude."

—A. A. MILNE

DATE _____

THE BEST MOMENT OF MY DAY: _____
_____
_____

THE WORST MOMENT OF MY DAY: _____
_____
_____

TODAY I FELT GRATEFUL FOR: _____
_____
_____
_____

DATE _____

THE BEST MOMENT OF MY DAY: _____
_____
_____

THE WORST MOMENT OF MY DAY: _____
_____
_____

TODAY I FELT GRATEFUL FOR: _____
_____
_____
_____

DATE _____

THE BEST MOMENT OF MY DAY: _____

_____

_____

THE WORST MOMENT OF MY DAY: _____

_____

_____

TODAY I FELT GRATEFUL FOR: _____

_____

_____

_____

DATE _____

THE BEST MOMENT OF MY DAY: _____

_____

_____

THE WORST MOMENT OF MY DAY: _____

_____

_____

TODAY I FELT GRATEFUL FOR: _____

_____

_____

DATE _____

THE BEST MOMENT OF MY DAY: _____

_____

_____

THE WORST MOMENT OF MY DAY: _____

_____

_____

TODAY I FELT GRATEFUL FOR: _____

_____

_____

_____

DATE _____

THE BEST MOMENT OF MY DAY: _____

_____

_____

THE WORST MOMENT OF MY DAY: _____

_____

_____

TODAY I FELT GRATEFUL FOR: _____

_____

_____

_____

DATE _____

THE BEST MOMENT OF MY DAY: _____

_____

_____

THE WORST MOMENT OF MY DAY: _____

_____

_____

TODAY I FELT GRATEFUL FOR: _____

_____

_____

_____

DATE _____

THE BEST MOMENT OF MY DAY: _____

_____

_____

THE WORST MOMENT OF MY DAY: _____

_____

_____

TODAY I FELT GRATEFUL FOR: _____

_____

_____

_____

DATE _____

THE BEST MOMENT OF MY DAY: _____

_____

_____

THE WORST MOMENT OF MY DAY: _____

_____

_____

TODAY I FELT GRATEFUL FOR: _____

_____

_____

_____

DATE _____

THE BEST MOMENT OF MY DAY: _____

_____

_____

THE WORST MOMENT OF MY DAY: _____

_____

_____

TODAY I FELT GRATEFUL FOR: _____

_____

_____

_____

DATE _____

THE BEST MOMENT OF MY DAY: _____

_____

_____

THE WORST MOMENT OF MY DAY: _____

_____

_____

TODAY I FELT GRATEFUL FOR: _____

_____

_____

_____

DATE _____

THE BEST MOMENT OF MY DAY: _____

_____

_____

THE WORST MOMENT OF MY DAY: _____

_____

_____

TODAY I FELT GRATEFUL FOR: _____

_____

_____

_____

"Be healthy and take care of yourself. But be happy with the beautiful things that make you, you."

—BEYONCÉ

DATE _____

THE BEST MOMENT OF MY DAY: _____

_____

_____

THE WORST MOMENT OF MY DAY: _____

_____

_____

TODAY I FELT GRATEFUL FOR: _____

_____

_____

_____

DATE _____

THE BEST MOMENT OF MY DAY: _____

_____

_____

THE WORST MOMENT OF MY DAY: _____

_____

_____

TODAY I FELT GRATEFUL FOR: _____

_____

_____

_____

DATE _____

THE BEST MOMENT OF MY DAY: _____
_____
_____

THE WORST MOMENT OF MY DAY: _____
_____
_____

TODAY I FELT GRATEFUL FOR: _____
_____
_____
_____

DATE _____

THE BEST MOMENT OF MY DAY: _____
_____
_____

THE WORST MOMENT OF MY DAY: _____
_____
_____

TODAY I FELT GRATEFUL FOR: _____
_____
_____

DATE _____

THE BEST MOMENT OF MY DAY: _____

_____

_____

THE WORST MOMENT OF MY DAY: _____

_____

_____

TODAY I FELT GRATEFUL FOR: _____

_____

_____

_____

DATE _____

THE BEST MOMENT OF MY DAY: _____

_____

_____

THE WORST MOMENT OF MY DAY: _____

_____

_____

TODAY I FELT GRATEFUL FOR: _____

_____

_____

_____

DATE _____

THE BEST MOMENT OF MY DAY: _____

_____

_____

THE WORST MOMENT OF MY DAY: _____

_____

_____

TODAY I FELT GRATEFUL FOR: _____

_____

_____

_____

DATE _____

THE BEST MOMENT OF MY DAY: _____

_____

_____

THE WORST MOMENT OF MY DAY: _____

_____

_____

TODAY I FELT GRATEFUL FOR: _____

_____

_____

_____

"Gratitude is an opener of locked-up blessings. Joy is what happens to us when we allow ourselves to recognize how good things really are."

—MARIANNE WILLIAMSON

DATE _____

THE BEST MOMENT OF MY DAY: _____
_____
_____

THE WORST MOMENT OF MY DAY: _____
_____
_____

TODAY I FELT GRATEFUL FOR: _____
_____
_____
_____

DATE _____

THE BEST MOMENT OF MY DAY: _____
_____
_____

THE WORST MOMENT OF MY DAY: _____
_____
_____

TODAY I FELT GRATEFUL FOR: _____
_____
_____
_____

DATE _____

THE BEST MOMENT OF MY DAY: _____
_____
_____

THE WORST MOMENT OF MY DAY: _____
_____
_____

TODAY I FELT GRATEFUL FOR: _____
_____
_____
_____

DATE _____

THE BEST MOMENT OF MY DAY: _____
_____
_____

THE WORST MOMENT OF MY DAY: _____
_____
_____

TODAY I FELT GRATEFUL FOR: _____
_____
_____

DATE _____

THE BEST MOMENT OF MY DAY: _____

_____

_____

THE WORST MOMENT OF MY DAY: _____

_____

_____

TODAY I FELT GRATEFUL FOR: _____

_____

_____

_____

DATE _____

THE BEST MOMENT OF MY DAY: _____

_____

_____

THE WORST MOMENT OF MY DAY: _____

_____

_____

TODAY I FELT GRATEFUL FOR: _____

_____

_____

_____

DATE _____

THE BEST MOMENT OF MY DAY: _____
_____
_____

THE WORST MOMENT OF MY DAY: _____
_____
_____

TODAY I FELT GRATEFUL FOR: _____
_____
_____
_____

DATE _____

THE BEST MOMENT OF MY DAY: _____
_____
_____

THE WORST MOMENT OF MY DAY: _____
_____
_____

TODAY I FELT GRATEFUL FOR: _____
_____
_____
_____

DATE _____

THE BEST MOMENT OF MY DAY: _____
_____
_____

THE WORST MOMENT OF MY DAY: _____
_____
_____

TODAY I FELT GRATEFUL FOR: _____
_____
_____
_____

DATE _____

THE BEST MOMENT OF MY DAY: _____
_____
_____

THE WORST MOMENT OF MY DAY: _____
_____
_____

TODAY I FELT GRATEFUL FOR: _____
_____
_____
_____

DATE _____

THE BEST MOMENT OF MY DAY: _____
_____
_____

THE WORST MOMENT OF MY DAY: _____
_____
_____

TODAY I FELT GRATEFUL FOR: _____
_____
_____
_____

DATE _____

THE BEST MOMENT OF MY DAY: _____
_____
_____

THE WORST MOMENT OF MY DAY: _____
_____
_____

TODAY I FELT GRATEFUL FOR: _____
_____
_____
_____

"**Acknowledging the good that you already have in your life is the foundation for all abundance.**"

—ECKHART TOLLE

DATE _____

THE BEST MOMENT OF MY DAY: _____

_____

_____

THE WORST MOMENT OF MY DAY: _____

_____

_____

TODAY I FELT GRATEFUL FOR: _____

_____

_____

_____

DATE _____

THE BEST MOMENT OF MY DAY: _____

_____

_____

THE WORST MOMENT OF MY DAY: _____

_____

_____

TODAY I FELT GRATEFUL FOR: _____

_____

_____

_____

DATE _____

THE BEST MOMENT OF MY DAY: _____
_____
_____

THE WORST MOMENT OF MY DAY: _____
_____
_____

TODAY I FELT GRATEFUL FOR: _____
_____
_____
_____

DATE _____

THE BEST MOMENT OF MY DAY: _____
_____
_____

THE WORST MOMENT OF MY DAY: _____
_____
_____

TODAY I FELT GRATEFUL FOR: _____
_____
_____

DATE _____

THE BEST MOMENT OF MY DAY: _____

_____

_____

THE WORST MOMENT OF MY DAY: _____

_____

_____

TODAY I FELT GRATEFUL FOR: _____

_____

_____

_____

DATE _____

THE BEST MOMENT OF MY DAY: _____

_____

_____

THE WORST MOMENT OF MY DAY: _____

_____

_____

TODAY I FELT GRATEFUL FOR: _____

_____

_____

DATE _____

THE BEST MOMENT OF MY DAY: _____

_____

_____

THE WORST MOMENT OF MY DAY: _____

_____

_____

TODAY I FELT GRATEFUL FOR: _____

_____

_____

_____

DATE _____

THE BEST MOMENT OF MY DAY: _____

_____

_____

THE WORST MOMENT OF MY DAY: _____

_____

_____

TODAY I FELT GRATEFUL FOR: _____

_____

_____

_____

"You must *choose* to be happy, grateful, and fulfilled. If you make that choice every single day, regardless of where you are or what's happening, you will be happy."

—RACHEL HOLLIS

DATE _____

THE BEST MOMENT OF MY DAY: _____
_____
_____

THE WORST MOMENT OF MY DAY: _____
_____
_____

TODAY I FELT GRATEFUL FOR: _____
_____
_____
_____

DATE _____

THE BEST MOMENT OF MY DAY: _____
_____
_____

THE WORST MOMENT OF MY DAY: _____
_____
_____

TODAY I FELT GRATEFUL FOR: _____
_____
_____

DATE _____

THE BEST MOMENT OF MY DAY: _____

_____

_____

THE WORST MOMENT OF MY DAY: _____

_____

_____

TODAY I FELT GRATEFUL FOR: _____

_____

_____

_____

DATE _____

THE BEST MOMENT OF MY DAY: _____

_____

_____

THE WORST MOMENT OF MY DAY: _____

_____

_____

TODAY I FELT GRATEFUL FOR: _____

_____

_____

_____

DATE _____

THE BEST MOMENT OF MY DAY: _____
_____
_____

THE WORST MOMENT OF MY DAY: _____
_____
_____

TODAY I FELT GRATEFUL FOR: _____
_____
_____
_____

DATE _____

THE BEST MOMENT OF MY DAY: _____
_____
_____

THE WORST MOMENT OF MY DAY: _____
_____
_____

TODAY I FELT GRATEFUL FOR: _____
_____
_____

DATE _____

THE BEST MOMENT OF MY DAY: _____
_____
_____

THE WORST MOMENT OF MY DAY: _____
_____
_____

TODAY I FELT GRATEFUL FOR: _____
_____
_____
_____

DATE _____

THE BEST MOMENT OF MY DAY: _____
_____
_____

THE WORST MOMENT OF MY DAY: _____
_____
_____

TODAY I FELT GRATEFUL FOR: _____
_____
_____

DATE _____

THE BEST MOMENT OF MY DAY: _____

_____

_____

THE WORST MOMENT OF MY DAY: _____

_____

_____

TODAY I FELT GRATEFUL FOR: _____

_____

_____

_____

DATE _____

THE BEST MOMENT OF MY DAY: _____

_____

_____

THE WORST MOMENT OF MY DAY: _____

_____

_____

TODAY I FELT GRATEFUL FOR: _____

_____

_____

_____

DATE _____

THE BEST MOMENT OF MY DAY: _____
_____
_____

THE WORST MOMENT OF MY DAY: _____
_____
_____

TODAY I FELT GRATEFUL FOR: _____
_____
_____
_____

DATE _____

THE BEST MOMENT OF MY DAY: _____
_____
_____

THE WORST MOMENT OF MY DAY: _____
_____
_____

TODAY I FELT GRATEFUL FOR: _____
_____
_____
_____

"Be thankful for what you have; you'll end up having more. If you concentrate on what you don't have, you will never, ever have enough."

—OPRAH WINFREY

DATE _____

THE BEST MOMENT OF MY DAY: _____

_____

_____

THE WORST MOMENT OF MY DAY: _____

_____

_____

TODAY I FELT GRATEFUL FOR: _____

_____

_____

_____

DATE _____

THE BEST MOMENT OF MY DAY: _____

_____

_____

THE WORST MOMENT OF MY DAY: _____

_____

_____

TODAY I FELT GRATEFUL FOR: _____

_____

_____

_____

DATE _____

THE BEST MOMENT OF MY DAY: _____

_____

_____

THE WORST MOMENT OF MY DAY: _____

_____

_____

TODAY I FELT GRATEFUL FOR: _____

_____

_____

_____

DATE _____

THE BEST MOMENT OF MY DAY: _____

_____

_____

THE WORST MOMENT OF MY DAY: _____

_____

_____

TODAY I FELT GRATEFUL FOR: _____

_____

_____

_____

DATE _____

THE BEST MOMENT OF MY DAY: _____
_____
_____

THE WORST MOMENT OF MY DAY: _____
_____
_____

TODAY I FELT GRATEFUL FOR: _____
_____
_____
_____

DATE _____

THE BEST MOMENT OF MY DAY: _____
_____
_____

THE WORST MOMENT OF MY DAY: _____
_____
_____

TODAY I FELT GRATEFUL FOR: _____
_____
_____
_____

DATE _____

THE BEST MOMENT OF MY DAY: _____
_____
_____

THE WORST MOMENT OF MY DAY: _____
_____
_____

TODAY I FELT GRATEFUL FOR: _____
_____
_____
_____

DATE _____

THE BEST MOMENT OF MY DAY: _____
_____
_____

THE WORST MOMENT OF MY DAY: _____
_____
_____

TODAY I FELT GRATEFUL FOR: _____
_____
_____
_____

"Gratitude unlocks all that's blocking us from really feeling truthful, really feeling authentic and vulnerable and happy."

—GABRIELLE BERNSTEIN

DATE _____

THE BEST MOMENT OF MY DAY: _____

_____

_____

THE WORST MOMENT OF MY DAY: _____

_____

_____

TODAY I FELT GRATEFUL FOR: _____

_____

_____

_____

DATE _____

THE BEST MOMENT OF MY DAY: _____

_____

_____

THE WORST MOMENT OF MY DAY: _____

_____

_____

TODAY I FELT GRATEFUL FOR: _____

_____

_____

_____

DATE _____

THE BEST MOMENT OF MY DAY: _____
_____
_____

THE WORST MOMENT OF MY DAY: _____
_____
_____

TODAY I FELT GRATEFUL FOR: _____
_____
_____
_____

DATE _____

THE BEST MOMENT OF MY DAY: _____
_____
_____

THE WORST MOMENT OF MY DAY: _____
_____
_____

TODAY I FELT GRATEFUL FOR: _____
_____
_____

DATE _____

THE BEST MOMENT OF MY DAY: _____

_____

_____

THE WORST MOMENT OF MY DAY: _____

_____

_____

TODAY I FELT GRATEFUL FOR: _____

_____

_____

_____

DATE _____

THE BEST MOMENT OF MY DAY: _____

_____

_____

THE WORST MOMENT OF MY DAY: _____

_____

_____

TODAY I FELT GRATEFUL FOR: _____

_____

_____

_____

DATE _____

THE BEST MOMENT OF MY DAY: _____
_____
_____

THE WORST MOMENT OF MY DAY: _____
_____
_____

TODAY I FELT GRATEFUL FOR: _____
_____
_____
_____

DATE _____

THE BEST MOMENT OF MY DAY: _____
_____
_____

THE WORST MOMENT OF MY DAY: _____
_____
_____

TODAY I FELT GRATEFUL FOR: _____
_____
_____
_____

DATE _____

THE BEST MOMENT OF MY DAY: _____
_____
_____

THE WORST MOMENT OF MY DAY: _____
_____
_____

TODAY I FELT GRATEFUL FOR: _____
_____
_____
_____

DATE _____

THE BEST MOMENT OF MY DAY: _____
_____
_____

THE WORST MOMENT OF MY DAY: _____
_____
_____

TODAY I FELT GRATEFUL FOR: _____
_____
_____
_____

DATE _____

THE BEST MOMENT OF MY DAY: _____

_____

_____

THE WORST MOMENT OF MY DAY: _____

_____

_____

TODAY I FELT GRATEFUL FOR: _____

_____

_____

_____

DATE _____

THE BEST MOMENT OF MY DAY: _____

_____

_____

THE WORST MOMENT OF MY DAY: _____

_____

_____

TODAY I FELT GRATEFUL FOR: _____

_____

_____

_____

"When I started counting my blessings, my whole life turned around."

—WILLIE NELSON

DATE _____

THE BEST MOMENT OF MY DAY: _____
_____
_____

THE WORST MOMENT OF MY DAY: _____
_____
_____

TODAY I FELT GRATEFUL FOR: _____
_____
_____
_____

DATE _____

THE BEST MOMENT OF MY DAY: _____
_____
_____

THE WORST MOMENT OF MY DAY: _____
_____
_____

TODAY I FELT GRATEFUL FOR: _____
_____
_____

DATE _____

THE BEST MOMENT OF MY DAY: _____

_____

_____

THE WORST MOMENT OF MY DAY: _____

_____

_____

TODAY I FELT GRATEFUL FOR: _____

_____

_____

_____

DATE _____

THE BEST MOMENT OF MY DAY: _____

_____

_____

THE WORST MOMENT OF MY DAY: _____

_____

_____

TODAY I FELT GRATEFUL FOR: _____

_____

_____

_____

DATE _____

THE BEST MOMENT OF MY DAY: _____
_____
_____

THE WORST MOMENT OF MY DAY: _____
_____
_____

TODAY I FELT GRATEFUL FOR: _____
_____
_____
_____

DATE _____

THE BEST MOMENT OF MY DAY: _____
_____
_____

THE WORST MOMENT OF MY DAY: _____
_____
_____

TODAY I FELT GRATEFUL FOR: _____
_____
_____
_____

DATE _____

THE BEST MOMENT OF MY DAY: _____

_____

_____

THE WORST MOMENT OF MY DAY: _____

_____

_____

TODAY I FELT GRATEFUL FOR: _____

_____

_____

_____

DATE _____

THE BEST MOMENT OF MY DAY: _____

_____

_____

THE WORST MOMENT OF MY DAY: _____

_____

_____

TODAY I FELT GRATEFUL FOR: _____

_____

_____

_____

"You can only enjoy something if you take a moment to appreciate it and pay attention to it."

—LILLY SINGH

DATE _____

THE BEST MOMENT OF MY DAY: _____
_____
_____

THE WORST MOMENT OF MY DAY: _____
_____
_____

TODAY I FELT GRATEFUL FOR: _____
_____
_____
_____

DATE _____

THE BEST MOMENT OF MY DAY: _____
_____
_____

THE WORST MOMENT OF MY DAY: _____
_____
_____

TODAY I FELT GRATEFUL FOR: _____
_____
_____
_____

DATE _____

THE BEST MOMENT OF MY DAY: _____

_____

_____

THE WORST MOMENT OF MY DAY: _____

_____

_____

TODAY I FELT GRATEFUL FOR: _____

_____

_____

_____

DATE _____

THE BEST MOMENT OF MY DAY: _____

_____

_____

THE WORST MOMENT OF MY DAY: _____

_____

_____

TODAY I FELT GRATEFUL FOR: _____

_____

_____

_____

DATE _____

THE BEST MOMENT OF MY DAY: _____

_____

_____

THE WORST MOMENT OF MY DAY: _____

_____

_____

TODAY I FELT GRATEFUL FOR: _____

_____

_____

_____

DATE _____

THE BEST MOMENT OF MY DAY: _____

_____

_____

THE WORST MOMENT OF MY DAY: _____

_____

_____

TODAY I FELT GRATEFUL FOR: _____

_____

_____

_____

DATE

THE BEST MOMENT OF MY DAY:

THE WORST MOMENT OF MY DAY:

TODAY I FELT GRATEFUL FOR:

DATE

THE BEST MOMENT OF MY DAY:

THE WORST MOMENT OF MY DAY:

TODAY I FELT GRATEFUL FOR:

DATE _____

THE BEST MOMENT OF MY DAY: _____
_____
_____

THE WORST MOMENT OF MY DAY: _____
_____
_____

TODAY I FELT GRATEFUL FOR: _____
_____
_____
_____

DATE _____

THE BEST MOMENT OF MY DAY: _____
_____
_____

THE WORST MOMENT OF MY DAY: _____
_____
_____

TODAY I FELT GRATEFUL FOR: _____
_____
_____

DATE _____

THE BEST MOMENT OF MY DAY: _____

_____

_____

THE WORST MOMENT OF MY DAY: _____

_____

_____

TODAY I FELT GRATEFUL FOR: _____

_____

_____

_____

DATE _____

THE BEST MOMENT OF MY DAY: _____

_____

_____

THE WORST MOMENT OF MY DAY: _____

_____

_____

TODAY I FELT GRATEFUL FOR: _____

_____

_____

_____

"I don't have to chase extraordinary moments to find happiness—it's right in front of me if I'm paying attention and practicing gratitude."

—BRENÉ BROWN

DATE _____

THE BEST MOMENT OF MY DAY: _____

_____

_____

THE WORST MOMENT OF MY DAY: _____

_____

_____

TODAY I FELT GRATEFUL FOR: _____

_____

_____

_____

DATE _____

THE BEST MOMENT OF MY DAY: _____

_____

_____

THE WORST MOMENT OF MY DAY: _____

_____

_____

TODAY I FELT GRATEFUL FOR: _____

_____

_____

_____

DATE _____

THE BEST MOMENT OF MY DAY: _____

_____

_____

THE WORST MOMENT OF MY DAY: _____

_____

_____

TODAY I FELT GRATEFUL FOR: _____

_____

_____

_____

DATE _____

THE BEST MOMENT OF MY DAY: _____

_____

_____

THE WORST MOMENT OF MY DAY: _____

_____

_____

TODAY I FELT GRATEFUL FOR: _____

_____

_____

_____

DATE _____

THE BEST MOMENT OF MY DAY: _____
_____
_____

THE WORST MOMENT OF MY DAY: _____
_____
_____

TODAY I FELT GRATEFUL FOR: _____
_____
_____
_____

DATE _____

THE BEST MOMENT OF MY DAY: _____
_____
_____

THE WORST MOMENT OF MY DAY: _____
_____
_____

TODAY I FELT GRATEFUL FOR: _____
_____
_____
_____

DATE _____

THE BEST MOMENT OF MY DAY: _____

_____

_____

THE WORST MOMENT OF MY DAY: _____

_____

_____

TODAY I FELT GRATEFUL FOR: _____

_____

_____

_____

DATE _____

THE BEST MOMENT OF MY DAY: _____

_____

_____

THE WORST MOMENT OF MY DAY: _____

_____

_____

TODAY I FELT GRATEFUL FOR: _____

_____

_____

"'Thank you' is the best prayer that anyone could say. I say that one a lot. Thank you expresses extreme gratitude, humility, understanding."

—ALICE WALKER

DATE _____

THE BEST MOMENT OF MY DAY: _____

_____

_____

THE WORST MOMENT OF MY DAY: _____

_____

_____

TODAY I FELT GRATEFUL FOR: _____

_____

_____

_____

DATE _____

THE BEST MOMENT OF MY DAY: _____

_____

_____

THE WORST MOMENT OF MY DAY: _____

_____

_____

TODAY I FELT GRATEFUL FOR: _____

_____

_____

_____

DATE _____

THE BEST MOMENT OF MY DAY: _____

_____

_____

THE WORST MOMENT OF MY DAY: _____

_____

_____

TODAY I FELT GRATEFUL FOR: _____

_____

_____

_____

DATE _____

THE BEST MOMENT OF MY DAY: _____

_____

_____

THE WORST MOMENT OF MY DAY: _____

_____

_____

TODAY I FELT GRATEFUL FOR: _____

_____

_____

_____

DATE _____

THE BEST MOMENT OF MY DAY: _____

_____

_____

THE WORST MOMENT OF MY DAY: _____

_____

_____

TODAY I FELT GRATEFUL FOR: _____

_____

_____

_____

DATE _____

THE BEST MOMENT OF MY DAY: _____

_____

_____

THE WORST MOMENT OF MY DAY: _____

_____

_____

TODAY I FELT GRATEFUL FOR: _____

_____

_____

_____

DATE _____

THE BEST MOMENT OF MY DAY: _____
_____
_____

THE WORST MOMENT OF MY DAY: _____
_____
_____

TODAY I FELT GRATEFUL FOR: _____
_____
_____
_____

DATE _____

THE BEST MOMENT OF MY DAY: _____
_____
_____

THE WORST MOMENT OF MY DAY: _____
_____
_____

TODAY I FELT GRATEFUL FOR: _____
_____
_____
_____

DATE _____

THE BEST MOMENT OF MY DAY: _____
_____
_____

THE WORST MOMENT OF MY DAY: _____
_____
_____

TODAY I FELT GRATEFUL FOR: _____
_____
_____
_____

DATE _____

THE BEST MOMENT OF MY DAY: _____
_____
_____

THE WORST MOMENT OF MY DAY: _____
_____
_____

TODAY I FELT GRATEFUL FOR: _____
_____
_____
_____

DATE _____

THE BEST MOMENT OF MY DAY: _____
_____
_____

THE WORST MOMENT OF MY DAY: _____
_____
_____

TODAY I FELT GRATEFUL FOR: _____
_____
_____
_____

DATE _____

THE BEST MOMENT OF MY DAY: _____
_____
_____

THE WORST MOMENT OF MY DAY: _____
_____
_____

TODAY I FELT GRATEFUL FOR: _____
_____
_____
_____

**"When you arise in
the morning, think of
what a precious privilege
it is to be alive–
to breathe, to think,
to enjoy, to love."**

—MARCUS AURELIUS

DATE _____

THE BEST MOMENT OF MY DAY: _____

_____

_____

THE WORST MOMENT OF MY DAY: _____

_____

_____

TODAY I FELT GRATEFUL FOR: _____

_____

_____

_____

DATE _____

THE BEST MOMENT OF MY DAY: _____

_____

_____

THE WORST MOMENT OF MY DAY: _____

_____

_____

TODAY I FELT GRATEFUL FOR: _____

_____

_____

_____

DATE _____

THE BEST MOMENT OF MY DAY: _____
_____
_____

THE WORST MOMENT OF MY DAY: _____
_____
_____

TODAY I FELT GRATEFUL FOR: _____
_____
_____
_____

DATE _____

THE BEST MOMENT OF MY DAY: _____
_____
_____

THE WORST MOMENT OF MY DAY: _____
_____
_____

TODAY I FELT GRATEFUL FOR: _____
_____
_____
_____

DATE _____

THE BEST MOMENT OF MY DAY: _____
_____
_____

THE WORST MOMENT OF MY DAY: _____
_____
_____

TODAY I FELT GRATEFUL FOR: _____
_____
_____
_____

DATE _____

THE BEST MOMENT OF MY DAY: _____
_____
_____

THE WORST MOMENT OF MY DAY: _____
_____
_____

TODAY I FELT GRATEFUL FOR: _____
_____
_____
_____

DATE _____

THE BEST MOMENT OF MY DAY: _____

_____

_____

THE WORST MOMENT OF MY DAY: _____

_____

_____

TODAY I FELT GRATEFUL FOR: _____

_____

_____

_____

DATE _____

THE BEST MOMENT OF MY DAY: _____

_____

_____

THE WORST MOMENT OF MY DAY: _____

_____

_____

TODAY I FELT GRATEFUL FOR: _____

_____

_____

_____

"Made a decision to enjoy life. No more uncontrollable anxiety. No more fruitless competition."

—LIZZO

DATE _____

THE BEST MOMENT OF MY DAY: _____

_____

_____

THE WORST MOMENT OF MY DAY: _____

_____

_____

TODAY I FELT GRATEFUL FOR: _____

_____

_____

_____

DATE _____

THE BEST MOMENT OF MY DAY: _____

_____

_____

THE WORST MOMENT OF MY DAY: _____

_____

_____

TODAY I FELT GRATEFUL FOR: _____

_____

_____

_____

DATE _____

THE BEST MOMENT OF MY DAY: _____
_____
_____

THE WORST MOMENT OF MY DAY: _____
_____
_____

TODAY I FELT GRATEFUL FOR: _____
_____
_____
_____

DATE _____

THE BEST MOMENT OF MY DAY: _____
_____
_____

THE WORST MOMENT OF MY DAY: _____
_____
_____

TODAY I FELT GRATEFUL FOR: _____
_____
_____

DATE _____

THE BEST MOMENT OF MY DAY: _____

_____

_____

THE WORST MOMENT OF MY DAY: _____

_____

_____

TODAY I FELT GRATEFUL FOR: _____

_____

_____

_____

DATE _____

THE BEST MOMENT OF MY DAY: _____

_____

_____

THE WORST MOMENT OF MY DAY: _____

_____

_____

TODAY I FELT GRATEFUL FOR: _____

_____

_____

_____

DATE _____

THE BEST MOMENT OF MY DAY: _____
_____
_____

THE WORST MOMENT OF MY DAY: _____
_____
_____

TODAY I FELT GRATEFUL FOR: _____
_____
_____
_____

DATE _____

THE BEST MOMENT OF MY DAY: _____
_____
_____

THE WORST MOMENT OF MY DAY: _____
_____
_____

TODAY I FELT GRATEFUL FOR: _____
_____
_____
_____

DATE _____

THE BEST MOMENT OF MY DAY: _____

_____

_____

THE WORST MOMENT OF MY DAY: _____

_____

_____

TODAY I FELT GRATEFUL FOR: _____

_____

_____

_____

DATE _____

THE BEST MOMENT OF MY DAY: _____

_____

_____

THE WORST MOMENT OF MY DAY: _____

_____

_____

TODAY I FELT GRATEFUL FOR: _____

_____

_____

DATE _____

THE BEST MOMENT OF MY DAY: _____

_____

_____

THE WORST MOMENT OF MY DAY: _____

_____

_____

TODAY I FELT GRATEFUL FOR: _____

_____

_____

_____

DATE _____

THE BEST MOMENT OF MY DAY: _____

_____

_____

THE WORST MOMENT OF MY DAY: _____

_____

_____

TODAY I FELT GRATEFUL FOR: _____

_____

_____

_____

"This a wonderful day. I've never seen this one before."

—MAYA ANGELOU

DATE _____

THE BEST MOMENT OF MY DAY: _____
_____
_____

THE WORST MOMENT OF MY DAY: _____
_____
_____

TODAY I FELT GRATEFUL FOR: _____
_____
_____
_____

DATE _____

THE BEST MOMENT OF MY DAY: _____
_____
_____

THE WORST MOMENT OF MY DAY: _____
_____
_____

TODAY I FELT GRATEFUL FOR: _____
_____
_____
_____

DATE _____

THE BEST MOMENT OF MY DAY: _____
_____
_____

THE WORST MOMENT OF MY DAY: _____
_____
_____

TODAY I FELT GRATEFUL FOR: _____
_____
_____
_____

DATE _____

THE BEST MOMENT OF MY DAY: _____
_____
_____

THE WORST MOMENT OF MY DAY: _____
_____
_____

TODAY I FELT GRATEFUL FOR: _____
_____
_____
_____

DATE _____

THE BEST MOMENT OF MY DAY: _____

_____

_____

THE WORST MOMENT OF MY DAY: _____

_____

_____

TODAY I FELT GRATEFUL FOR: _____

_____

_____

_____

DATE _____

THE BEST MOMENT OF MY DAY: _____

_____

_____

THE WORST MOMENT OF MY DAY: _____

_____

_____

TODAY I FELT GRATEFUL FOR: _____

_____

_____

_____

DATE _____

THE BEST MOMENT OF MY DAY: _____

_____

_____

THE WORST MOMENT OF MY DAY: _____

_____

_____

TODAY I FELT GRATEFUL FOR: _____

_____

_____

_____

DATE _____

THE BEST MOMENT OF MY DAY: _____

_____

_____

THE WORST MOMENT OF MY DAY: _____

_____

_____

TODAY I FELT GRATEFUL FOR: _____

_____

_____

_____

"Cultivate the habit of being grateful for every good thing that comes to you, and to give thanks continuously. And because all things have contributed to your advancement, you should include all things in your gratitude."

—RALPH WALDO EMERSON

DATE _____

THE BEST MOMENT OF MY DAY: _____

_____

_____

THE WORST MOMENT OF MY DAY: _____

_____

_____

TODAY I FELT GRATEFUL FOR: _____

_____

_____

_____

DATE _____

THE BEST MOMENT OF MY DAY: _____

_____

_____

THE WORST MOMENT OF MY DAY: _____

_____

_____

TODAY I FELT GRATEFUL FOR: _____

_____

_____

_____

DATE _____

THE BEST MOMENT OF MY DAY: _____
_____
_____

THE WORST MOMENT OF MY DAY: _____
_____
_____

TODAY I FELT GRATEFUL FOR: _____
_____
_____
_____

DATE _____

THE BEST MOMENT OF MY DAY: _____
_____
_____

THE WORST MOMENT OF MY DAY: _____
_____
_____

TODAY I FELT GRATEFUL FOR: _____
_____
_____
_____

DATE _____

THE BEST MOMENT OF MY DAY: _____

_____

_____

THE WORST MOMENT OF MY DAY: _____

_____

_____

TODAY I FELT GRATEFUL FOR: _____

_____

_____

_____

DATE _____

THE BEST MOMENT OF MY DAY: _____

_____

_____

THE WORST MOMENT OF MY DAY: _____

_____

_____

TODAY I FELT GRATEFUL FOR: _____

_____

_____

_____

DATE _____

THE BEST MOMENT OF MY DAY: _____

_____

_____

THE WORST MOMENT OF MY DAY: _____

_____

_____

TODAY I FELT GRATEFUL FOR: _____

_____

_____

_____

DATE _____

THE BEST MOMENT OF MY DAY: _____

_____

_____

THE WORST MOMENT OF MY DAY: _____

_____

_____

TODAY I FELT GRATEFUL FOR: _____

_____

_____

_____

DATE _____

THE BEST MOMENT OF MY DAY: _____

_____

_____

THE WORST MOMENT OF MY DAY: _____

_____

_____

TODAY I FELT GRATEFUL FOR: _____

_____

_____

_____

DATE _____

THE BEST MOMENT OF MY DAY: _____

_____

_____

THE WORST MOMENT OF MY DAY: _____

_____

_____

TODAY I FELT GRATEFUL FOR: _____

_____

_____

_____

DATE _____

THE BEST MOMENT OF MY DAY: _____
_____
_____

THE WORST MOMENT OF MY DAY: _____
_____
_____

TODAY I FELT GRATEFUL FOR: _____
_____
_____
_____

DATE _____

THE BEST MOMENT OF MY DAY: _____
_____
_____

THE WORST MOMENT OF MY DAY: _____
_____
_____

TODAY I FELT GRATEFUL FOR: _____
_____
_____
_____

"Sunny days wouldn't be special if it wasn't for rain. Joy wouldn't feel so good if it wasn't for pain."

—CURTIS "50 CENT" JACKSON

DATE _____

THE BEST MOMENT OF MY DAY: _____
_____
_____

THE WORST MOMENT OF MY DAY: _____
_____
_____

TODAY I FELT GRATEFUL FOR: _____
_____
_____
_____

DATE _____

THE BEST MOMENT OF MY DAY: _____
_____
_____

THE WORST MOMENT OF MY DAY: _____
_____
_____

TODAY I FELT GRATEFUL FOR: _____
_____
_____
_____

DATE _____

THE BEST MOMENT OF MY DAY: _____

_____

_____

THE WORST MOMENT OF MY DAY: _____

_____

_____

TODAY I FELT GRATEFUL FOR: _____

_____

_____

_____

DATE _____

THE BEST MOMENT OF MY DAY: _____

_____

_____

THE WORST MOMENT OF MY DAY: _____

_____

_____

TODAY I FELT GRATEFUL FOR: _____

_____

_____

_____

DATE _____

THE BEST MOMENT OF MY DAY: _____

_____

_____

THE WORST MOMENT OF MY DAY: _____

_____

_____

TODAY I FELT GRATEFUL FOR: _____

_____

_____

_____

DATE _____

THE BEST MOMENT OF MY DAY: _____

_____

_____

THE WORST MOMENT OF MY DAY: _____

_____

_____

TODAY I FELT GRATEFUL FOR: _____

_____

_____

_____

DATE _____

THE BEST MOMENT OF MY DAY: _____

_____

_____

THE WORST MOMENT OF MY DAY: _____

_____

_____

TODAY I FELT GRATEFUL FOR: _____

_____

_____

_____

DATE _____

THE BEST MOMENT OF MY DAY: _____

_____

_____

THE WORST MOMENT OF MY DAY: _____

_____

_____

TODAY I FELT GRATEFUL FOR: _____

_____

_____

_____

"In the external scheme of things, shining moments are as brief as the twinkling of an eye, yet such twinklings are what eternity is made of– moments when we human beings can say 'I love you,' 'I'm proud of you,' 'I forgive you,' 'I'm grateful for you.' That's what eternity is made of: invisible, imperishable good stuff."

—FRED "MISTER" ROGERS

DATE _____

THE BEST MOMENT OF MY DAY: _____

_____

_____

THE WORST MOMENT OF MY DAY: _____

_____

_____

TODAY I FELT GRATEFUL FOR: _____

_____

_____

_____

DATE _____

THE BEST MOMENT OF MY DAY: _____

_____

_____

THE WORST MOMENT OF MY DAY: _____

_____

_____

TODAY I FELT GRATEFUL FOR: _____

_____

_____

_____

DATE _____

THE BEST MOMENT OF MY DAY: _____

_____

_____

THE WORST MOMENT OF MY DAY: _____

_____

_____

TODAY I FELT GRATEFUL FOR: _____

_____

_____

_____

DATE _____

THE BEST MOMENT OF MY DAY: _____

_____

_____

THE WORST MOMENT OF MY DAY: _____

_____

_____

TODAY I FELT GRATEFUL FOR: _____

_____

_____

_____

DATE _____

THE BEST MOMENT OF MY DAY: _____
_____
_____

THE WORST MOMENT OF MY DAY: _____
_____
_____

TODAY I FELT GRATEFUL FOR: _____
_____
_____
_____

DATE _____

THE BEST MOMENT OF MY DAY: _____
_____
_____

THE WORST MOMENT OF MY DAY: _____
_____
_____

TODAY I FELT GRATEFUL FOR: _____
_____
_____
_____

DATE _____

THE BEST MOMENT OF MY DAY: _____

_____

_____

THE WORST MOMENT OF MY DAY: _____

_____

_____

TODAY I FELT GRATEFUL FOR: _____

_____

_____

_____

DATE _____

THE BEST MOMENT OF MY DAY: _____

_____

_____

THE WORST MOMENT OF MY DAY: _____

_____

_____

TODAY I FELT GRATEFUL FOR: _____

_____

_____

_____

DATE _____

THE BEST MOMENT OF MY DAY: _____
_____
_____

THE WORST MOMENT OF MY DAY: _____
_____
_____

TODAY I FELT GRATEFUL FOR: _____
_____
_____
_____

DATE _____

THE BEST MOMENT OF MY DAY: _____
_____
_____

THE WORST MOMENT OF MY DAY: _____
_____
_____

TODAY I FELT GRATEFUL FOR: _____
_____
_____

DATE _____

THE BEST MOMENT OF MY DAY: _____

_____

_____

THE WORST MOMENT OF MY DAY: _____

_____

_____

TODAY I FELT GRATEFUL FOR: _____

_____

_____

_____

DATE _____

THE BEST MOMENT OF MY DAY: _____

_____

_____

THE WORST MOMENT OF MY DAY: _____

_____

_____

TODAY I FELT GRATEFUL FOR: _____

_____

_____

_____

"Gratitude is looking
on the brighter side of
the life, even if it means
hurting your eyes."

—ELLEN DEGENERES

DATE _____

THE BEST MOMENT OF MY DAY: _____

_____

_____

THE WORST MOMENT OF MY DAY: _____

_____

_____

TODAY I FELT GRATEFUL FOR: _____

_____

_____

_____

DATE _____

THE BEST MOMENT OF MY DAY: _____

_____

_____

THE WORST MOMENT OF MY DAY: _____

_____

_____

TODAY I FELT GRATEFUL FOR: _____

_____

_____

_____

DATE _____

THE BEST MOMENT OF MY DAY: _____

_____

_____

THE WORST MOMENT OF MY DAY: _____

_____

_____

TODAY I FELT GRATEFUL FOR: _____

_____

_____

_____

DATE _____

THE BEST MOMENT OF MY DAY: _____

_____

_____

THE WORST MOMENT OF MY DAY: _____

_____

_____

TODAY I FELT GRATEFUL FOR: _____

_____

_____

_____

DATE _____

THE BEST MOMENT OF MY DAY: _____

_____

_____

THE WORST MOMENT OF MY DAY: _____

_____

_____

TODAY I FELT GRATEFUL FOR: _____

_____

_____

_____

DATE _____

THE BEST MOMENT OF MY DAY: _____

_____

_____

THE WORST MOMENT OF MY DAY: _____

_____

_____

TODAY I FELT GRATEFUL FOR: _____

_____

_____

_____

DATE _____

THE BEST MOMENT OF MY DAY: _____

_____

_____

THE WORST MOMENT OF MY DAY: _____

_____

_____

TODAY I FELT GRATEFUL FOR: _____

_____

_____

_____

DATE _____

THE BEST MOMENT OF MY DAY: _____

_____

_____

THE WORST MOMENT OF MY DAY: _____

_____

_____

TODAY I FELT GRATEFUL FOR: _____

_____

_____

_____

"Don't ever make decisions based on fear. Make decisions based on hope and possibility."

—MICHELLE OBAMA

DATE _____

THE BEST MOMENT OF MY DAY: _____

_____

_____

THE WORST MOMENT OF MY DAY: _____

_____

_____

TODAY I FELT GRATEFUL FOR: _____

_____

_____

_____

DATE _____

THE BEST MOMENT OF MY DAY: _____

_____

_____

THE WORST MOMENT OF MY DAY: _____

_____

_____

TODAY I FELT GRATEFUL FOR: _____

_____

_____

_____

DATE _____

THE BEST MOMENT OF MY DAY: _____

_____

_____

THE WORST MOMENT OF MY DAY: _____

_____

_____

TODAY I FELT GRATEFUL FOR: _____

_____

_____

_____

DATE _____

THE BEST MOMENT OF MY DAY: _____

_____

_____

THE WORST MOMENT OF MY DAY: _____

_____

_____

TODAY I FELT GRATEFUL FOR: _____

_____

_____

DATE _____

THE BEST MOMENT OF MY DAY: _____

_____

_____

THE WORST MOMENT OF MY DAY: _____

_____

_____

TODAY I FELT GRATEFUL FOR: _____

_____

_____

_____

DATE _____

THE BEST MOMENT OF MY DAY: _____

_____

_____

THE WORST MOMENT OF MY DAY: _____

_____

_____

TODAY I FELT GRATEFUL FOR: _____

_____

_____

_____

DATE _____

THE BEST MOMENT OF MY DAY: _____

_____

_____

THE WORST MOMENT OF MY DAY: _____

_____

_____

TODAY I FELT GRATEFUL FOR: _____

_____

_____

_____

DATE _____

THE BEST MOMENT OF MY DAY: _____

_____

_____

THE WORST MOMENT OF MY DAY: _____

_____

_____

TODAY I FELT GRATEFUL FOR: _____

_____

_____

_____

DATE _____

THE BEST MOMENT OF MY DAY: _____

_____

_____

THE WORST MOMENT OF MY DAY: _____

_____

_____

TODAY I FELT GRATEFUL FOR: _____

_____

_____

_____

DATE _____

THE BEST MOMENT OF MY DAY: _____

_____

_____

THE WORST MOMENT OF MY DAY: _____

_____

_____

TODAY I FELT GRATEFUL FOR: _____

_____

_____

_____

DATE _____

THE BEST MOMENT OF MY DAY: _____
_____
_____

THE WORST MOMENT OF MY DAY: _____
_____
_____

TODAY I FELT GRATEFUL FOR: _____
_____
_____
_____

DATE _____

THE BEST MOMENT OF MY DAY: _____
_____
_____

THE WORST MOMENT OF MY DAY: _____
_____
_____

TODAY I FELT GRATEFUL FOR: _____
_____
_____
_____

"When we focus on our gratitude, the tide of disappointment goes out and the tide of love rushes in."

—KRISTIN ARMSTRONG

DATE _____

THE BEST MOMENT OF MY DAY: _____

_____

_____

THE WORST MOMENT OF MY DAY: _____

_____

_____

TODAY I FELT GRATEFUL FOR: _____

_____

_____

_____

DATE _____

THE BEST MOMENT OF MY DAY: _____

_____

_____

THE WORST MOMENT OF MY DAY: _____

_____

_____

TODAY I FELT GRATEFUL FOR: _____

_____

_____

_____

DATE _____

THE BEST MOMENT OF MY DAY: _____

_____

_____

THE WORST MOMENT OF MY DAY: _____

_____

_____

TODAY I FELT GRATEFUL FOR: _____

_____

_____

_____

DATE _____

THE BEST MOMENT OF MY DAY: _____

_____

_____

THE WORST MOMENT OF MY DAY: _____

_____

_____

TODAY I FELT GRATEFUL FOR: _____

_____

_____

_____

DATE _____

THE BEST MOMENT OF MY DAY: _____
_____
_____

THE WORST MOMENT OF MY DAY: _____
_____
_____

TODAY I FELT GRATEFUL FOR: _____
_____
_____
_____

DATE _____

THE BEST MOMENT OF MY DAY: _____
_____
_____

THE WORST MOMENT OF MY DAY: _____
_____
_____

TODAY I FELT GRATEFUL FOR: _____
_____
_____
_____

DATE _____

THE BEST MOMENT OF MY DAY: _____

_____

_____

THE WORST MOMENT OF MY DAY: _____

_____

_____

TODAY I FELT GRATEFUL FOR: _____

_____

_____

_____

DATE _____

THE BEST MOMENT OF MY DAY: _____

_____

_____

THE WORST MOMENT OF MY DAY: _____

_____

_____

TODAY I FELT GRATEFUL FOR: _____

_____

_____

_____

"Keeping your body healthy is an expression of gratitude to the whole cosmos–the trees, the clouds, everything."

—THICH NHAT HANH

DATE _____

THE BEST MOMENT OF MY DAY: _____
_____
_____

THE WORST MOMENT OF MY DAY: _____
_____
_____

TODAY I FELT GRATEFUL FOR: _____
_____
_____
_____

DATE _____

THE BEST MOMENT OF MY DAY: _____
_____
_____

THE WORST MOMENT OF MY DAY: _____
_____
_____

TODAY I FELT GRATEFUL FOR: _____
_____
_____
_____

DATE _____

THE BEST MOMENT OF MY DAY: _____

_____

_____

THE WORST MOMENT OF MY DAY: _____

_____

_____

TODAY I FELT GRATEFUL FOR: _____

_____

_____

_____

DATE _____

THE BEST MOMENT OF MY DAY: _____

_____

_____

THE WORST MOMENT OF MY DAY: _____

_____

_____

TODAY I FELT GRATEFUL FOR: _____

_____

_____

_____

DATE _____

THE BEST MOMENT OF MY DAY: _____

_____

_____

THE WORST MOMENT OF MY DAY: _____ .

_____

_____

TODAY I FELT GRATEFUL FOR: _____

_____

_____

_____

DATE _____

THE BEST MOMENT OF MY DAY: _____

_____

_____

THE WORST MOMENT OF MY DAY: _____

_____

_____

TODAY I FELT GRATEFUL FOR: _____

_____

_____

_____

DATE _____

THE BEST MOMENT OF MY DAY: _____

_____

_____

THE WORST MOMENT OF MY DAY: _____

_____

_____

TODAY I FELT GRATEFUL FOR: _____

_____

_____

_____

DATE _____

THE BEST MOMENT OF MY DAY: _____

_____

_____

THE WORST MOMENT OF MY DAY: _____

_____

_____

TODAY I FELT GRATEFUL FOR: _____

_____

_____

_____

DATE _____

THE BEST MOMENT OF MY DAY: _____

_____

_____

THE WORST MOMENT OF MY DAY: _____

_____

_____

TODAY I FELT GRATEFUL FOR: _____

_____

_____

_____

DATE _____

THE BEST MOMENT OF MY DAY: _____

_____

_____

THE WORST MOMENT OF MY DAY: _____

_____

_____

TODAY I FELT GRATEFUL FOR: _____

_____

_____

_____

DATE _____

THE BEST MOMENT OF MY DAY: _____
_____
_____

THE WORST MOMENT OF MY DAY: _____
_____
_____

TODAY I FELT GRATEFUL FOR: _____
_____
_____
_____

DATE _____

THE BEST MOMENT OF MY DAY: _____
_____
_____

THE WORST MOMENT OF MY DAY: _____
_____
_____

TODAY I FELT GRATEFUL FOR: _____
_____
_____
_____

"Got no checkbooks, got no banks. Still I'd like to express my thanks—I've got the sun in the mornin' and the moon at night."

—IRVING BERLIN

DATE _____

THE BEST MOMENT OF MY DAY: _____

_____

_____

THE WORST MOMENT OF MY DAY: _____

_____

_____

TODAY I FELT GRATEFUL FOR: _____

_____

_____

_____

DATE _____

THE BEST MOMENT OF MY DAY: _____

_____

_____

THE WORST MOMENT OF MY DAY: _____

_____

_____

TODAY I FELT GRATEFUL FOR: _____

_____

_____

DATE _____

THE BEST MOMENT OF MY DAY: _____
_____
_____

THE WORST MOMENT OF MY DAY: _____
_____
_____

TODAY I FELT GRATEFUL FOR: _____
_____
_____
_____

DATE _____

THE BEST MOMENT OF MY DAY: _____
_____
_____

THE WORST MOMENT OF MY DAY: _____
_____
_____

TODAY I FELT GRATEFUL FOR: _____
_____
_____
_____

DATE _____

THE BEST MOMENT OF MY DAY: _____
_____
_____

THE WORST MOMENT OF MY DAY: _____
_____
_____

TODAY I FELT GRATEFUL FOR: _____
_____
_____
_____

DATE _____

THE BEST MOMENT OF MY DAY: _____
_____
_____

THE WORST MOMENT OF MY DAY: _____
_____
_____

TODAY I FELT GRATEFUL FOR: _____
_____
_____
_____

DATE _____

THE BEST MOMENT OF MY DAY: _____

_____

_____

THE WORST MOMENT OF MY DAY: _____

_____

_____

TODAY I FELT GRATEFUL FOR: _____

_____

_____

_____

DATE _____

THE BEST MOMENT OF MY DAY: _____

_____

_____

THE WORST MOMENT OF MY DAY: _____

_____

_____

TODAY I FELT GRATEFUL FOR: _____

_____

_____

_____

"Today I define success by the fluidity with which I transcend emotional land mines and choose joy and gratitude instead."

—RUPAUL

DATE _____

THE BEST MOMENT OF MY DAY: _____
_____
_____

THE WORST MOMENT OF MY DAY: _____
_____
_____

TODAY I FELT GRATEFUL FOR: _____
_____
_____
_____

DATE _____

THE BEST MOMENT OF MY DAY: _____
_____
_____

THE WORST MOMENT OF MY DAY: _____
_____
_____

TODAY I FELT GRATEFUL FOR: _____
_____
_____
_____

DATE _____

THE BEST MOMENT OF MY DAY: _____
_____
_____

THE WORST MOMENT OF MY DAY: _____
_____
_____

TODAY I FELT GRATEFUL FOR: _____
_____
_____
_____

DATE _____

THE BEST MOMENT OF MY DAY: _____
_____
_____

THE WORST MOMENT OF MY DAY: _____
_____
_____

TODAY I FELT GRATEFUL FOR: _____
_____
_____
_____

DATE _____

THE BEST MOMENT OF MY DAY: _____
_____
_____

THE WORST MOMENT OF MY DAY: _____
_____
_____

TODAY I FELT GRATEFUL FOR: _____
_____
_____
_____

DATE _____

THE BEST MOMENT OF MY DAY: _____
_____
_____

THE WORST MOMENT OF MY DAY: _____
_____
_____

TODAY I FELT GRATEFUL FOR: _____
_____
_____
_____

DATE _____

THE BEST MOMENT OF MY DAY: _____

_____

_____

THE WORST MOMENT OF MY DAY: _____

_____

_____

TODAY I FELT GRATEFUL FOR: _____

_____

_____

_____

DATE _____

THE BEST MOMENT OF MY DAY: _____

_____

_____

THE WORST MOMENT OF MY DAY: _____

_____

_____

TODAY I FELT GRATEFUL FOR: _____

_____

_____

DATE _____

THE BEST MOMENT OF MY DAY: _____

_____

_____

THE WORST MOMENT OF MY DAY: _____

_____

_____

TODAY I FELT GRATEFUL FOR: _____

_____

_____

_____

DATE _____

THE BEST MOMENT OF MY DAY: _____

_____

_____

THE WORST MOMENT OF MY DAY: _____

_____

_____

TODAY I FELT GRATEFUL FOR: _____

_____

_____

_____

DATE _____

THE BEST MOMENT OF MY DAY: _____
_____
_____

THE WORST MOMENT OF MY DAY: _____
_____
_____

TODAY I FELT GRATEFUL FOR: _____
_____
_____
_____

DATE _____

THE BEST MOMENT OF MY DAY: _____
_____
_____

THE WORST MOMENT OF MY DAY: _____
_____
_____

TODAY I FELT GRATEFUL FOR: _____
_____
_____
_____

"**Sometimes I need only to stand wherever I am to be blessed.**"

—MARY OLIVER

DATE _____

THE BEST MOMENT OF MY DAY: _____
_____
_____

THE WORST MOMENT OF MY DAY: _____
_____
_____

TODAY I FELT GRATEFUL FOR: _____
_____
_____
_____

DATE _____

THE BEST MOMENT OF MY DAY: _____
_____
_____

THE WORST MOMENT OF MY DAY: _____
_____
_____

TODAY I FELT GRATEFUL FOR: _____
_____
_____
_____

DATE _____

THE BEST MOMENT OF MY DAY: _____

_____

_____

THE WORST MOMENT OF MY DAY: _____

_____

_____

TODAY I FELT GRATEFUL FOR: _____

_____

_____

_____

DATE _____

THE BEST MOMENT OF MY DAY: _____

_____

_____

THE WORST MOMENT OF MY DAY: _____

_____

_____

TODAY I FELT GRATEFUL FOR: _____

_____

_____

_____

DATE _____

THE BEST MOMENT OF MY DAY: _____
_____
_____

THE WORST MOMENT OF MY DAY: _____
_____
_____

TODAY I FELT GRATEFUL FOR: _____
_____
_____
_____

DATE _____

THE BEST MOMENT OF MY DAY: _____
_____
_____

THE WORST MOMENT OF MY DAY: _____
_____
_____

TODAY I FELT GRATEFUL FOR: _____
_____
_____
_____

DATE _____

THE BEST MOMENT OF MY DAY: _____
_____
_____

THE WORST MOMENT OF MY DAY: _____
_____
_____

TODAY I FELT GRATEFUL FOR: _____
_____
_____
_____

DATE _____

THE BEST MOMENT OF MY DAY: _____
_____
_____

THE WORST MOMENT OF MY DAY: _____
_____
_____

TODAY I FELT GRATEFUL FOR: _____
_____
_____
_____

"I am eternally grateful [...] for my knack of finding in great books, some of them very funny books, reason enough to feel honored to be alive, no matter what else may be going on."

—KURT VONNEGUT

DATE _____

THE BEST MOMENT OF MY DAY: _____

_____

_____

THE WORST MOMENT OF MY DAY: _____

_____

_____

TODAY I FELT GRATEFUL FOR: _____

_____

_____

_____

DATE _____

THE BEST MOMENT OF MY DAY: _____

_____

_____

THE WORST MOMENT OF MY DAY: _____

_____

_____

TODAY I FELT GRATEFUL FOR: _____

_____

_____

_____

DATE _____

THE BEST MOMENT OF MY DAY: _____
_____
_____

THE WORST MOMENT OF MY DAY: _____
_____
_____

TODAY I FELT GRATEFUL FOR: _____
_____
_____
_____

DATE _____

THE BEST MOMENT OF MY DAY: _____
_____
_____

THE WORST MOMENT OF MY DAY: _____
_____
_____

TODAY I FELT GRATEFUL FOR: _____
_____
_____
_____

DATE _____

THE BEST MOMENT OF MY DAY: _____
_____
_____

THE WORST MOMENT OF MY DAY: _____
_____
_____

TODAY I FELT GRATEFUL FOR: _____
_____
_____
_____

DATE _____

THE BEST MOMENT OF MY DAY: _____
_____
_____

THE WORST MOMENT OF MY DAY: _____
_____
_____

TODAY I FELT GRATEFUL FOR: _____
_____
_____
_____

DATE _____

THE BEST MOMENT OF MY DAY: _____
_____
_____

THE WORST MOMENT OF MY DAY: _____
_____
_____

TODAY I FELT GRATEFUL FOR: _____
_____
_____
_____

DATE _____

THE BEST MOMENT OF MY DAY: _____
_____
_____

THE WORST MOMENT OF MY DAY: _____
_____
_____

TODAY I FELT GRATEFUL FOR: _____
_____
_____
_____

DATE _____

THE BEST MOMENT OF MY DAY: _____

_____

_____

THE WORST MOMENT OF MY DAY: _____

_____

_____

TODAY I FELT GRATEFUL FOR: _____

_____

_____

_____

DATE _____

THE BEST MOMENT OF MY DAY: _____

_____

_____

THE WORST MOMENT OF MY DAY: _____

_____

_____

TODAY I FELT GRATEFUL FOR: _____

_____

_____

_____

DATE _____

THE BEST MOMENT OF MY DAY: _____

_____

_____

THE WORST MOMENT OF MY DAY: _____

_____

_____

TODAY I FELT GRATEFUL FOR: _____

_____

_____

_____

DATE _____

THE BEST MOMENT OF MY DAY: _____

_____

_____

THE WORST MOMENT OF MY DAY: _____

_____

_____

TODAY I FELT GRATEFUL FOR: _____

_____

_____

_____

"Gratitude and appreciating where you are is very important to me."

—TIMOTHÉE CHALAMET

DATE _____

THE BEST MOMENT OF MY DAY: _____
_____
_____

THE WORST MOMENT OF MY DAY: _____
_____
_____

TODAY I FELT GRATEFUL FOR: _____
_____
_____
_____

DATE _____

THE BEST MOMENT OF MY DAY: _____
_____
_____

THE WORST MOMENT OF MY DAY: _____
_____
_____

TODAY I FELT GRATEFUL FOR: _____
_____
_____
_____

DATE _____

THE BEST MOMENT OF MY DAY: _____

_____

_____

THE WORST MOMENT OF MY DAY: _____

_____

_____

TODAY I FELT GRATEFUL FOR: _____

_____

_____

_____

DATE _____

THE BEST MOMENT OF MY DAY: _____

_____

_____

THE WORST MOMENT OF MY DAY: _____

_____

_____

TODAY I FELT GRATEFUL FOR: _____

_____

_____

_____

DATE _____

THE BEST MOMENT OF MY DAY: _____
_____
_____

THE WORST MOMENT OF MY DAY: _____
_____
_____

TODAY I FELT GRATEFUL FOR: _____
_____
_____
_____

DATE _____

THE BEST MOMENT OF MY DAY: _____
_____
_____

THE WORST MOMENT OF MY DAY: _____
_____
_____

TODAY I FELT GRATEFUL FOR: _____
_____
_____
_____

DATE _____

THE BEST MOMENT OF MY DAY: _____
_____
_____

THE WORST MOMENT OF MY DAY: _____
_____
_____

TODAY I FELT GRATEFUL FOR: _____
_____
_____
_____

DATE _____

THE BEST MOMENT OF MY DAY: _____
_____
_____

THE WORST MOMENT OF MY DAY: _____
_____
_____

TODAY I FELT GRATEFUL FOR: _____
_____
_____
_____

"I have noticed that the Universe loves Gratitude. The more grateful you are, the more goodies you get."

—LOUISE HAY

DATE _____

THE BEST MOMENT OF MY DAY: _____

_____

_____

THE WORST MOMENT OF MY DAY: _____

_____

_____

TODAY I FELT GRATEFUL FOR: _____

_____

_____

_____

DATE _____

THE BEST MOMENT OF MY DAY: _____

_____

_____

THE WORST MOMENT OF MY DAY: _____

_____

_____

TODAY I FELT GRATEFUL FOR: _____

_____

_____

_____

DATE _____

THE BEST MOMENT OF MY DAY: _____
_____
_____

THE WORST MOMENT OF MY DAY: _____
_____
_____

TODAY I FELT GRATEFUL FOR: _____
_____
_____
_____

DATE _____

THE BEST MOMENT OF MY DAY: _____
_____
_____

THE WORST MOMENT OF MY DAY: _____
_____
_____

TODAY I FELT GRATEFUL FOR: _____
_____
_____
_____

DATE _____

THE BEST MOMENT OF MY DAY: _____
_____
_____

THE WORST MOMENT OF MY DAY: _____
_____
_____

TODAY I FELT GRATEFUL FOR: _____
_____
_____
_____

DATE _____

THE BEST MOMENT OF MY DAY: _____
_____
_____

THE WORST MOMENT OF MY DAY: _____
_____
_____

TODAY I FELT GRATEFUL FOR: _____
_____
_____
_____

DATE _____

THE BEST MOMENT OF MY DAY: _____

_____

_____

THE WORST MOMENT OF MY DAY: _____

_____

_____

TODAY I FELT GRATEFUL FOR: _____

_____

_____

_____

DATE _____

THE BEST MOMENT OF MY DAY: _____

_____

_____

THE WORST MOMENT OF MY DAY: _____

_____

_____

TODAY I FELT GRATEFUL FOR: _____

_____

_____

_____

DATE _____

THE BEST MOMENT OF MY DAY: _____
_____
_____

THE WORST MOMENT OF MY DAY: _____
_____
_____

TODAY I FELT GRATEFUL FOR: _____
_____
_____
_____

DATE _____

THE BEST MOMENT OF MY DAY: _____
_____
_____

THE WORST MOMENT OF MY DAY: _____
_____
_____

TODAY I FELT GRATEFUL FOR: _____
_____
_____
_____

DATE _____

THE BEST MOMENT OF MY DAY: _____
_____
_____

THE WORST MOMENT OF MY DAY: _____
_____
_____

TODAY I FELT GRATEFUL FOR: _____
_____
_____
_____

DATE _____

THE BEST MOMENT OF MY DAY: _____
_____
_____

THE WORST MOMENT OF MY DAY: _____
_____
_____

TODAY I FELT GRATEFUL FOR: _____
_____
_____
_____

"You can always, always give something, even if it is only kindness!"

—ANNE FRANK

DATE _____

THE BEST MOMENT OF MY DAY: _____

_____

_____

THE WORST MOMENT OF MY DAY: _____

_____

_____

TODAY I FELT GRATEFUL FOR: _____

_____

_____

_____

DATE _____

THE BEST MOMENT OF MY DAY: _____

_____

_____

THE WORST MOMENT OF MY DAY: _____

_____

_____

TODAY I FELT GRATEFUL FOR: _____

_____

_____

_____

DATE _____

THE BEST MOMENT OF MY DAY: _____

_____

_____

THE WORST MOMENT OF MY DAY: _____

_____

_____

TODAY I FELT GRATEFUL FOR: _____

_____

_____

_____

DATE _____

THE BEST MOMENT OF MY DAY: _____

_____

_____

THE WORST MOMENT OF MY DAY: _____

_____

_____

TODAY I FELT GRATEFUL FOR: _____

_____

_____

_____

DATE _____

THE BEST MOMENT OF MY DAY: _____
_____
_____

THE WORST MOMENT OF MY DAY: _____
_____
_____

TODAY I FELT GRATEFUL FOR: _____
_____
_____
_____

DATE _____

THE BEST MOMENT OF MY DAY: _____
_____
_____

THE WORST MOMENT OF MY DAY: _____
_____
_____

TODAY I FELT GRATEFUL FOR: _____
_____
_____
_____

DATE _____

THE BEST MOMENT OF MY DAY: _____

_____

_____

THE WORST MOMENT OF MY DAY: _____

_____

_____

TODAY I FELT GRATEFUL FOR: _____

_____

_____

_____

DATE _____

THE BEST MOMENT OF MY DAY: _____

_____

_____

THE WORST MOMENT OF MY DAY: _____

_____

_____

TODAY I FELT GRATEFUL FOR: _____

_____

_____

_____

"The root of joy is gratefulness. . . . For it is not joy that makes us grateful; it is gratitude that makes us joyful."

—BROTHER DAVID STEINDL-RAST

DATE _____

THE BEST MOMENT OF MY DAY: _____
_____
_____

THE WORST MOMENT OF MY DAY: _____
_____
_____

TODAY I FELT GRATEFUL FOR: _____
_____
_____
_____

DATE _____

THE BEST MOMENT OF MY DAY: _____
_____
_____

THE WORST MOMENT OF MY DAY: _____
_____
_____

TODAY I FELT GRATEFUL FOR: _____
_____
_____
_____

DATE _____

THE BEST MOMENT OF MY DAY: _____
_____
_____

THE WORST MOMENT OF MY DAY: _____
_____
_____

TODAY I FELT GRATEFUL FOR: _____
_____
_____
_____

DATE _____

THE BEST MOMENT OF MY DAY: _____
_____
_____

THE WORST MOMENT OF MY DAY: _____
_____
_____

TODAY I FELT GRATEFUL FOR: _____
_____
_____
_____

DATE _____

THE BEST MOMENT OF MY DAY: _____

_____

_____

THE WORST MOMENT OF MY DAY: _____

_____

_____

TODAY I FELT GRATEFUL FOR: _____

_____

_____

_____

DATE _____

THE BEST MOMENT OF MY DAY: _____

_____

_____

THE WORST MOMENT OF MY DAY: _____

_____

_____

TODAY I FELT GRATEFUL FOR: _____

_____

_____

_____

DATE _____

THE BEST MOMENT OF MY DAY: _____

_____

_____

THE WORST MOMENT OF MY DAY: _____

_____

_____

TODAY I FELT GRATEFUL FOR: _____

_____

_____

_____

DATE _____

THE BEST MOMENT OF MY DAY: _____

_____

_____

THE WORST MOMENT OF MY DAY: _____

_____

_____

TODAY I FELT GRATEFUL FOR: _____

_____

_____

DATE _____

THE BEST MOMENT OF MY DAY: _____

_____

_____

THE WORST MOMENT OF MY DAY: _____

_____

_____

TODAY I FELT GRATEFUL FOR: _____

_____

_____

_____

DATE _____

THE BEST MOMENT OF MY DAY: _____

_____

_____

THE WORST MOMENT OF MY DAY: _____

_____

_____

TODAY I FELT GRATEFUL FOR: _____

_____

_____

_____

DATE _____

THE BEST MOMENT OF MY DAY: _____
_____
_____

THE WORST MOMENT OF MY DAY: _____
_____
_____

TODAY I FELT GRATEFUL FOR: _____
_____
_____
_____

DATE _____

THE BEST MOMENT OF MY DAY: _____
_____
_____

THE WORST MOMENT OF MY DAY: _____
_____
_____

TODAY I FELT GRATEFUL FOR: _____
_____
_____
_____

DATE _____

THE BEST MOMENT OF MY DAY: _____
_____

THE WORST MOMENT OF MY DAY: _____
_____

TODAY I FELT GRATEFUL FOR: _____
_____
_____
_____

DATE _____

THE BEST MOMENT OF MY DAY: _____
_____
_____

THE WORST MOMENT OF MY DAY: _____
_____

TODAY I FELT GRATEFUL FOR: _____
_____
_____

DATE _____

THE BEST MOMENT OF MY DAY: _____

_____

_____

THE WORST MOMENT OF MY DAY: _____

_____

_____

TODAY I FELT GRATEFUL FOR: _____

_____

_____

_____

DATE _____

THE BEST MOMENT OF MY DAY: _____

_____

_____

THE WORST MOMENT OF MY DAY: _____

_____

_____

TODAY I FELT GRATEFUL FOR: _____

_____

_____

_____

"The point is not to
pay back kindness
but to pass it on."

—JULIA ALVAREZ

Printed in China

SPRUCE BOOKS with colophon is a registered trademark of Penguin Random House LLC

26 25 24 23 22   9 8 7 6 5 4 3

Editor: Sharyn Rosart
Production editor: Jill Saginario
Cover illustration and lettering: Alicia Terry
Cover design: Lynne Yeamans and Alicia Terry
Interior design: Alicia Terry

ISBN: 978-1-63217-346-1

Sasquatch Books
1325 Fourth Avenue, Suite 1025
Seattle, WA 98101

SasquatchBooks.com

MIX
Paper from
responsible sources
FSC® C001701

FSC
www.fsc.org